DO WHEN YOU'RE DEAD?

WHAT WILL YOU DO WHEN YOU'RE DEAD?

ED HARDING

BRIDGE LOGOS

Newberry, FL 32669

Bridge-Logos
Newberry, FL 32669

What Will You Do When You're Dead?
By Ed Harding

Printed in the United States of America.

Library of Congress Catalog Card Number:
2022947863

International Standard Book Number:
978-1-61036-282-5

Cover/Interior design by Kent Jensen | knail.com

BP 12/2022

CHAPTERS

CHAPTER ONE

WHAT WILL YOU DO WHEN YOU'RE DEAD?

SO, YOU'RE READING this short book, maybe out of curiosity, or maybe you've never really thought about death, as it's not anyone's favorite subject. But it will happen, sooner or later, maybe suddenly, as in a car accident, or a diagnosis of cancer, or maybe after a long and fruitful life. Many people simply ignore it and don't even make a will, but we really ought to know rather more about it than we do. Then we can prepare properly.

My observation over many years is that there are three basic views:

The first is, when I' m dead I'm dead. That's it. Six feet under. I simply cease to exist in any conscious state. This view is often expressed as 'I'm not religious' and a non-religious funeral takes place.

The second is, nobody really knows what happens next.

If there's a God, maybe there is, maybe there isn't, nobody knows for sure, and, if there is a Heaven, maybe there is, maybe there isn't, nobody knows for sure, then God must be nice and everyone gets to go there!

It's a nice thought, but is it true?

The third view is, that it is possible to know for sure from what the Bible reveals to us, so you have to decide if you believe the biblical narrative and what Jesus said or not.

So, what can we discover about each of these views? The information I'm going to share is all based on the biblical world view and can be checked by the references given, taken from the New King James Bible. Where a contemporary version makes the text easier to understand the New Living Translation has been used and marked NLT.

When I'm dead, I'm dead. I won't be doing anything!

That would be true if all you are is a set of molecules and cells, and the physical body either decomposes (burial) or is burned (cremation). What if there's more to you? What if you are actually a spiritual being who lives in a physical body, and it's only the physical body that dies?

> *But there is a spirit within people, the breath of the Almighty within them, that makes them intelligent.* (Job 32:8 NLT)

> *The human spirit can endure a sick body but who can bear a crushed spirit?* (Proverbs 18:14 NLT)

> *None of us can hold back our spirit from departing. None of us has the power to prevent the day of our death.* (Ecclesiastes 8:8 NLT)

> *The spirit will return to God who gave it.* (Ecclesiastes 12:7)

Then we have examples in the gospels such as Luke 8:52–55.

A little girl had clearly died. Verse 53 says the people knew she was dead for sure. Yet verse 55 states that her spirit returned, and she arose immediately.

When Stephen was stoned (Acts 7:59) he cried out, *"Lord Jesus, receive my spirit."*

Finally, James 2:26 tells us clearly *"the body without the spirit is dead."*

We are actually all spiritual beings, living in a physical body, which will die, then the spirit (the real us) will return to God. We will see later on what happens then.

If God exists and Heaven exists everyone gets to go there.

This view is surprisingly common and is based on the idea that God must be kind and merciful and if we've done our best/ been a good person, then what more could be expected of us?

It's called *universalism* and is based on the idea that because Jesus died for all mankind, therefore all mankind has been redeemed, so all are saved.

Unfortunately, it's not what the Bible teaches and Jesus Himself said.

So, what happens after the spirit returns to God?

> *And just as each person is destined to die once, and after that comes judgement...*
> (Hebrews 9:27 NLT)

God has given to each human being the wonderful gift of life on an incredibly beautiful earth with all its animals, birds, flowers, trees, fish, rivers and mountains, but when we die there is an accounting for how we have lived and how we have followed God's laws, as Romans 14:10 clearly states:

> *For we shall all stand before the judgement seat of Christ.* (Romans 14:10)

> *So, then each one of us shall give account of himself to God.* (Romans 14:12)

CHAPTER TWO

WHAT IS SIN AND WHAT IS THE TEST?

HOW DOES THIS work? It's a little bit like an exam, only the problem is the pass mark is 100% and it's impossible to pass.

The person who might get 90% has done better than someone who got say 50% but both fail.

That's why Romans 3:23 states, *"all have sinned and fall short of the glory of God."*

Basically, it's whether we have kept the Law

that God gave to Israel, which we call the Ten Commandments, listed in Exodus 20.

Here they are in full because if you have broken any of them you are a lawbreaker in God's eyes, and we'll see what that means.

You shall have no other gods before Me.

You shall not make for yourself a carved image—any likeness of anything that is in heaven above, or that is in the earth beneath, or that is in the water under the earth; you shall not bow down to them nor serve them. For I, the Lord your God, am a jealous God, visiting the iniquity of the fathers upon the children to the third and fourth generations of those who hate Me, but showing mercy to thousands, to those who love Me and keep My commandments.

You shall not take the name of the Lord your God in vain, for the Lord will not hold him guiltless who takes His name in vain.

Remember the Sabbath day, to keep it holy. Six days you shall labor and do all your work. But the seventh day is the Sabbath of the Lord your God. In it you shall do no work; you, nor your son, nor your daughter, nor your male servant, nor your female servant, nor your cattle, nor your stranger who is within your gates. For in six days the Lord made the heavens and the earth, the sea, and all that is in them, and rested the seventh day. Therefore, the Lord blessed the Sabbath day and hallowed it.

Honor your father and your mother, that your days may be long upon the land which the Lord your God is giving you.

You shall not murder.

You shall not commit adultery.

You shall not steal.

You shall not bear false witness against your neighbor.

You shall not covet your neighbor's house; you shall not covet your neighbor's wife, nor his male servant, nor his female servant, nor his ox, nor his donkey, nor anything that is your neighbor's.

So that's the heart of the problem. We have all broken God's laws, sometimes summarized as "the Law". This is where it is important to understand what Jesus did for us, and what we are required to do in return. He became a mediator between us and God in paying the price for our sin that we should have paid for breaking God's Law.

John 3:16–17 puts it this way:

> *For God so loved the world that He gave His only begotten Son, that whoever believes in Him should not perish but have everlasting life, For God did not send His Son into the world to condemn the world, but that the world through Him might be saved.*
>
> *He who believes in Him is not condemned; but he who does not believe is condemned already, because he has not believed in the name of the only begotten Son of God. And this is the condemnation, that light has come into the world, and men loved darkness rather than light, because their deeds were evil.*

Jesus says (Matthew 7:13):

> *"Enter by the narrow gate: for wide is the gate and broad is the way that leads to destruction, and there are many who go in by it. Because narrow is the gate and*

> *difficult is the way that leads to life, and there are few who find it."*

What does believing in Jesus then mean? It doesn't mean believing in God. The devil believes in God!

It means believing that Jesus as the Son of God lived a sinless life on the earth and sacrificed Himself on the cross at Calvary for our sins, so that we could be forgiven, and apply that to our lives.

After the crucifixion Peter preached to the crowd (Acts 2:36–39) that God raised Jesus from the dead.

> *"Therefore, let all the house of Israel know assuredly that God has made this Jesus, whom you crucified, both Lord and Christ."*

When they heard this they were cut to the heart, and said to Peter and the rest of the apostles, *"Men and brethren, what shall we do?"*

Then Peter said to them, *"Repent, and let every one of you be baptized in the name of Jesus Christ for the remission of sins; and you shall receive the gift of the Holy Spirit. For the promise is to you and to your children, and to all who are afar off, as many as the Lord our God will call."*

So that's what we are required to do: Repent, believe and be baptized.

Repentance is fundamentally acknowledging that we are all sinners, and some people need to repent for specific sins they know they've committed. The good news is that there is no sin that God cannot and will not forgive other than rejection of His Son Jesus.

Repentance simply means changing direction to be a follower of Jesus.

Believe is trusting that Jesus died for you personally on the cross as your substitute, i.e., in your place.

Personal faith is required, i.e., it is a proactive decision.

Being baptized is a post conversion experience and personal decision so cannot be done on your behalf by someone else. The Greek word *baptizo* not only means to fully immerse in water but also to totally identify with something else. So, we are baptized into Christ, into His death and resurrection. It's a decision you can make even as a child, but not a baby. It cannot be made for you by someone else. They can dedicate you as a baby to God, but you have to choose to be baptized, just as you have to choose to be born again and saved.

Jesus said:

> *"I tell you the truth, unless you are born again, you cannot see the Kingdom of God".* (John 3:3 NLT)

> *"I assure you, no one can enter the Kingdom of God without being born of water and the Spirit. Humans can only reproduce human life, but the Holy Spirit gives birth to spiritual life. So don't be surprised when I say, 'You must be born again.'"* (John 3:5–7 NLT)

So here we have it. We must be reborn spiritually into the Kingdom of Heaven. Unless a man, or woman, is born again they cannot enter the Kingdom of God. Believing in God, going to church, doing good deeds, none of that will give you entry into the Kingdom of God. You must be born again!

The question is, are you? If you are you will know for sure because the Holy Spirit will be in you. That's what it means, Spirit gives birth to spirit—your spirit comes alive (John 3:8). You will definitely know!

Hopefully by now we've established that salvation/ going to Heaven is far from automatic and universal. It requires a specific personal commitment to trust in Christ as your personal savior. Then we can look at what that means and what awaits us.

CHAPTER THREE

THE RESURRECTION

THE FIRST PRINCIPLE to establish is that Jesus Himself rose from the dead.

Paul describes it like this:

> *For if the dead do not rise, then Christ is not risen. And if Christ is not risen, your faith is futile; you are still in your sins!*
>
> (1 Corinthians 15:16)

However, the truth, and indeed the heart of the Christian gospel, is that God raised Jesus from the dead and will raise us also.

> *He presented Himself alive after His suffering by many infallible proofs, being seen by them during forty days and speaking of the things pertaining to the kingdom of God.* (Acts 1:3)

> *I passed on to you what was most important and what had also been passed on to me. Christ died for our sins, just as the Scriptures said. He was buried, and he was raised from the dead on the third day, just as the Scriptures said. He was seen by Peter and then by the Twelve. After that, he was seen by more than 500 of his followers at one time, most of whom are still alive though some have died. Then he was seen by James and later by all the apostles.* (1 Corinthians 15:3–7 NLT)

The real question is not whether we are raised from the dead, but what kind of resurrection it will be. The Bible talks about two different resurrections, the just (believers in Christ) and unbelievers.

It is worth at this point saying something about the truth, because we live in a postmodern society where many claim the truth is what you believe it to be. But that is not the case.

Something is either true or not true. The Bible is either true or not true. It doesn't depend on whether you believe it.

Everything Jesus said was, and is true, whether you believe it or not. We ignore the Word of God at our peril, because it contains so many warnings.

> *How shall we escape if we neglect so great a salvation?* (Hebrews 2:3)

Let's now look at the two resurrections, best summarized by the words of Jesus Himself:

> *"I tell you the truth, those who listen to my message and believe in God who sent me have eternal life. They will never be condemned for their sins, but have already passed from death to life. And I assure you that the time is coming, when the dead will hear my voice—the voice of the Son of God. And those who listen will live. The Father has life in himself, and he has granted that same life-giving power to his Son. And he has given him authority to judge everyone because he is the Son of Man. Don't be surprised! Indeed, the time is coming when all the*

dead in their graves will hear the voice of God's Son and they will rise again. Those who have done good will rise to experience eternal life and those who have continued in evil will rise to experience judgment."

(John 5:24–29 NLT)

Jesus also tells us:

"And I tell you this, you must give an account on judgment day for every idle word you speak. The words you say will either acquit you or condemn you."

(Matthew 12:36 NLT)

So, there you have it spelt out.

For we shall all stand before the judgement seat of Christ. For it is written:

"As I live, says the Lord,
Every knee shall bow to Me,
And every tongue shall confess to God."
So, then each of us shall give account of himself to God. (Romans 14:10–12)

For we must all appear before the judgement seat of Christ, that each one may receive the things done in the body, according to what he has done, whether good or bad. (2 Corinthians 5:10)

It is a fearful thing to fall into the hands of the living God. (Hebrews 10:31)

How will you face this prospect, which cannot be avoided if the Bible is true? The big question won't be whether you were a good person or not, did your best, went to church etc... The big question will be whether you trusted in Christ as your personal savior or not. That is what determines your eternal destiny.

That is what salvation means, or being saved. What you are actually saved from is the consequence of paying the price for your own sin.

You face God either as savior or as a judge, and He simply underlines the decision you have taken in this life, to accept or reject Christ.

That makes it a pretty important decision, in fact the most important decision of your life here on earth!

God is not angry at you nor wanting to punish you. Quite the opposite and has prepared this wonderful way of paying for our sins by trusting that Jesus paid the price we should have paid and deserved. He Himself said:

> *"I am the way, the truth and the life. No one comes to the Father except through Me."* (John 14:6)

> *Nor is there salvation in any other, for there is no other name under heaven given among men by which we must be saved.* (Acts 4:12)

That key decision will determine your eternal destiny. We will now examine what the Bible says about Heaven and Hell, which are not allegorical but real places. That makes it pretty important to know what the Bible reveals about them. Then we will see why Jesus will return to the earth to establish His Kingdom (there are more prophecies about His second coming than His first), and why God creates a new Heaven and a new Earth. It's not all bad news, certainly not for the believer and in fact a truly amazing future awaits those of us who are.

One of our difficulties understanding all this is the assumption that any afterlife is somehow a continuation of life on earth, which is not the case.

The early Christians wanted to know so Paul told them:

> *But someone may ask, "How will the dead be raised? What kind of bodies will they have? What a foolish question! When you put a seed into the ground, it doesn't grow into a plant unless it dies first. And what you put in the ground is not the plant that will grow, but only a bare seed of wheat or whatever you are planting. Then God gives it the new body he wants it to have.*
>
> (1 Corinthians 15:35–38 NLT)

It is the same with the resurrection of the dead. Our earthly bodies are planted in the ground when we die, but they will be raised to live forever. Our bodies are buried in brokenness, but they will be raised in glory.

They are buried in weakness, but they will be raised in strength. They are buried as natural human bodies, but they will be raised as spiritual bodies. For just as there are natural bodies there are spiritual bodies.

The Scriptures tell us, *"The first man, Adam, became a living person." But the last Adam—that is Christ—is a life-giving Spirit. What comes first is the natural body, then the spiritual body comes later.*

(1 Corinthians 15:42–46 NLT)

If you don't like your current physical body, be assured you will be getting a brand-new spiritual body that will be just perfect for you. Whether you die young or old, for the believer, a perfect new body awaits you.

Paul continues:

> *Then when our dying bodies have been transformed into bodies that will never die, this Scripture will be fulfilled: Death is swallowed up in victory.*
>
> *O death, where is your victory?*
>
> *O death, where is your sting?*
>
> *For sin is the sting that results in death, and the law gives sin its power. But thank God! He gives us victory over sin and death through our Lord Jesus Christ.*
>
> (1 Corinthians 15:54–57 NLT)

For the believer it's a new body and a new destiny. For the unbeliever, i.e., all who reject

God's free gift of salvation, it's a different prospect when:

> *the Lord Jesus appears from heaven. He will come with his mighty angels, in flaming fire, bringing judgment on those who don't know God, and on those who refuse to obey the good news of our Lord Jesus.*
>
> *These shall be punished with eternal destruction, forever separated from the Lord and from his glorious power.*
>
> (2 Thessalonians 1:7–9 NLT)

Although this is a reference to the return of the Lord, which we'll see later, it clearly establishes the principle of punishment for those who reject the gospel and God's gift of forgiveness and salvation.

So, there are two possible destinations, Heaven or Hell, and we need to see what the Bible says about each.

CHAPTER FOUR

HEAVEN, IS IT A REAL PLACE?

WELL, FIRST OF all the Bible talks about three heavens.

The first is basically Earth's atmosphere, what we can see from Planet Earth.

The second is what we refer to as space, where the sun, moon, planets and stars are called heavenly bodies.

The third heaven is beyond space and is what we think about when we use the term, Heaven. We aren't told much about it but Paul writes about his vision:

> *I know a man in Christ who fourteen years ago—whether in the body I do not know, or whether out of the body I do not know, God knows—such a one was caught up to the third heaven. And I know such a man—whether in the body or out of the body I do not know, God knows—how he was caught up into Paradise and heard inexpressible words, which it is not lawful for a man to utter.*
>
> (2 Corinthians 12:1–4)

A number of people have had near death experiences and visions of being drawn up to a bright light as if in a tunnel, and there are many books recording these experiences.

Paul also reminds the Corinthian Church:

> *"No eye has seen, no ear had heard,*
> *and no mind has imagined*
> *what God has prepared*
> *for those who love him."*
> *But it was to us that God revealed these things by his Spirit.*
>
> (1 Corinthians 2:9–10 NLT)

In other words, it is possible to receive dreams and visions of Heaven, if you are a believer. It's not that common and there is always a reason, such as the stoning of Stephen:

> *But he, being full of the Holy Spirit, gazed into heaven and saw the glory of God, and Jesus standing at the right hand of God, and said, "Look! I see the heavens opened and the Son of Man standing at the right hand of God!"* (Acts 8: 55–56).

It is also possible to have visions of Hell, which we'll cover later.

What else can we know? The Pharisees asked Jesus about a woman who could have been married to seven different men.

Jesus answered and said to them, *"Are you not therefore mistaken, because you do not know the Scriptures nor the power of God? For when they rise from the dead they neither marry, nor are given in marriage, but are like angels in heaven."* (Mark 12:24–25)

That's particularly good news if you've been married multiple times or been divorced! We will instead have new angelic bodies, free from any health issues.

There are over five hundred references to Heaven or the heavens in the Bible. You are probably most familiar with the beginning of the Lord's Prayer:

> *Our Father, who art in Heaven*
>
> (Matthew 6:9 KJV)

Heaven is the realm of the Father, Jesus the Son, plus also the angels.

Jesus told Nathaniel:

> *"I tell you the truth, you will all see heaven open and the angels of God going up and down on the Son of Man, the one who is the stairway between heaven and earth."*
>
> (John 1:51 NLT)

Jesus talked about laying up treasure in Heaven and rewards for the faithful:

> *"Blessed are you when they revile and persecute you, and say all kinds of evil against you falsely for My sake. Rejoice and be exceedingly glad, for great is your reward in heaven, for so they persecuted the prophets who were before you."*
>
> (Matthew 5:11–12)

> *"He who receives a prophet in the name of a prophet shall receive a prophet's reward.*

> *And he who receives a righteous man shall receive a righteous man's reward. And whoever gives one of these little ones only a cup of water in the name of a disciple, assuredly, I say to you, he shall by no means lose his reward."*
>
> (Matthew 10:41–42)

It's clear that Heaven is not somewhere where everyone is the same, because there is a structure of rewards and indeed crowns. God is totally just and fair and we will each receive what we deserve. It would be quite wrong for a Chinese pastor who has spent years in prison to receive the same reward as someone who has not paid any real price in the free Western world. There are many who have served God under terrible persecution and remained faithful. God will give them their reward.

To establish our reward requires our works in this life to be tested by fire:

For no one can lay any foundation other than the one we already have—Jesus Christ.

> *Anyone builds on that foundation may use a variety of materials—gold, silver, jewels, wood, hay, or straw. But on the*

> *judgment day, fire will reveal what kind of work each builder has done. The fire will show if a person's work has any value. If the work survives, that builder will receive a reward. But if the work is burned up, the builder will suffer great loss. The builder will be saved, but like someone barely escaping through a wall of flames.* (1 Corinthians 3:11–15 NLT)

This tells us that you can be a believer, be born again and actually end up with no reward because you didn't build on your faith and serve God, however you won't lose your salvation. You make it to Heaven, but with nothing to show for it.

There is also clear a recognition of particular people who God honors for their service to Him, by giving them crowns. We're actually told more about the crowns than the rewards. Here's a list of them:

A crown of righteousness

> *And now the prize awaits me—the crown of righteousness, which the Lord, the righteous Judge, will give me on the day of his return. And the prize is not just for me*

> *but for all who eagerly look forward to his appearing.* (2 Timothy 4:8 NLT)

A crown of glory

> *When the Chief Shepherd appears, you will receive the crown of glory that does not fade away.* (1 Peter 5:4)

A crown of life

> *God blesses those who patiently endure testing and temptation. Afterward they will receive the crown of life that God has promised to those who love him.*
> (James 1:12 NLT)

> *Be faithful unto death and I will give you the crown of life* (the martyr's crown).
> (Revelation 2:10)

There will clearly be an honoring and recognition of faithful believers.

Much of what we're told about Heaven comes in the context of the Book of Revelation, which outlines the timescale for the return of the Lord, and God's final plan for us. Jesus also told many parables, what the Kingdom of Heaven is like.

"The kingdom of heaven is like a mustard seed, which a man took and sowed in his field, which indeed is the least of all the seeds; but when it is grown it is greater than the herbs and becomes a tree, so that the birds of the air come and nest in its branches." (Matthew 13:31–32)

"The Kingdom of Heaven is like the yeast a woman used in making bread. Even though she only put a little yeast in three measures of flour, it permeated every part of the dough." (Matthew 13:33 NLT)

"Again, the kingdom of heaven is like treasure hidden in a field, which a man found and hid; and for joy over it he goes and sells all that he has and buys that field." (Matthew 13:44)

"Again, the kingdom of heaven is like a merchant seeking beautiful pearls, who, when he had found one pearl of great price, went and sold all that he had and bought it." (Matthew 13:45)

"Again the Kingdom of Heaven is like a fishing net that was thrown into the water and caught fish of every kind. When the

> *net was full, they dragged it up onto the shore, sat down, and sorted the good fish into crates, but threw the bad ones away. That is the way it will be at the end of the world. The angels will come and separate the wicked people from the righteous, throwing the wicked into the fiery furnace, where there will be weeping and gnashing of teeth."* (Matthew 13:47–50 NLT)

There is clearly going to be a separation. We will look later at what the close of the age or the end of the world means and what to expect on the earth, however we now need to see what the Bible tells us about Hell.

Is it a real place or just used as a euphemism for something terrible—Hell on earth? Many people simply do not believe it's a real place and definitely do not believe they might go there! Hence the age-old question why a God of Love would send anyone there. But He is also a God of holiness, righteousness and justice and His character cannot ignore sin and the breaking of His laws.

CHAPTER FIVE

WHAT DO WE KNOW ABOUT HELL?

THERE ARE FOUR basic words used and translated as Hell:

1. Sheol, which literally means the unseen state.
2. Hades, which literally means the unseen world.
3. Gehenna, based on the valley of Hinnom outside Jerusalem.
4. Tartarus, a subterranean place of punishment lower than Hades.

So, what did Jesus say? Quite a lot about Hell!

He talked about the rich man and Lazarus, who both died.

> *So it was that the beggar died, and was carried by the angels to Abraham's bosom. The rich man also died and was buried. And being in torments in Hades (Hell) he lifted up his eyes and saw Abraham afar off, and Lazarus in his bosom.*

Then he cried and said, *"Father Abraham, have mercy on me, and send Lazarus that he may dip the tip of his finger in water and cool my tongue; for I am tormented in this flame."* (Luke 16:22–24)

He was told that it's not possible as there's a great gulf fixed so no one can cross it. His response was to ask him to go to his father's house and warn his brothers. The reply is very significant:

> *"They have Moses and the prophets; let them hear them."*

And he said, *"No, Father Abraham; but if one goes to them from the dead they will repent."*

But he said to him, *"If they do not hear Moses and the prophets, neither will they be persuaded though one rise from the dead."*

That's true of today and prophetic because some people still will not believe the Bible, or the gospel, even though Jesus rose from the dead.

We have enough warnings from Scripture.

> *"And do not fear those who kill the body but cannot kill the soul. But rather fear Him who is able to destroy both soul and body in hell* (Gehenna)*."*
>
> (Matthew 10:28)

> *"Woe to you, scribes and Pharisees, hypocrites! Because you build the tombs of the prophets and adorn the monuments of the righteous, and say,*
>
> *"If we had lived in the days of our fathers, we would not have been partakers with them in the blood of the prophets."*
>
> *Therefore you are witnesses against yourselves that you are sons of those who murdered the prophets. Fill up then the measure of your fathers' guilt. Serpents,*

> *brood of vipers! How can you escape the condemnation of hell* (Gehenna)*?"*
>
> (Matthew 23:29–33)

> *"But whoever causes one of these little ones who believe in Me to stumble, it would be better for him if a millstone were hung around his neck, and he were thrown into the sea. If your hand causes you to sin, cut it off. It is better for you to enter life maimed, rather than having two hands, to go to hell* (Gehenna)*, into the fire that shall never be quenched—where*
>
> *"Their worm does not die*
> *And the fire is not quenched."*
>
> (Mark 9:42–44)

> *"Woe to you, scribes and Pharisees! For you travel land and sea to win one proselyte, and when he is won, you make him twice as much a son of hell* (Gehenna) *as yourselves."* (Matthew 23:15)

The reference to Tartarus in 2 Peter links up with the Book of Revelation and God's final judgement of the fallen angels (demons) and the devil himself ultimately thrown into the Lake of Fire.

> *For if God did not spare the angels who sinned, but cast them down to hell (Tartarus).......* (2 Peter 2:4)

What is clear is that there is a place of punishment for those who reject God's way of salvation through faith in Jesus. However many comedians mock it and cartoonists draw pictures of the devil with horns and a trident, the actual reality is that it's a place to be avoided at all costs! I want to tackle some of the reasons people reject the gospel, and will inevitably face the judgment of God as a consequence.

Paul addresses some of these in his letter to the Corinthian Church.

> *For the message of the cross is foolishness to those who are perishing, but to us who are being saved it is the power of God.*
> (1 Corinthians 1:18)

To some people it seems foolish that God would allow Jesus to be crucified. Surely a more rational approach would be that good people go to Heaven and bad people don't. Isn't doing good and being a good person a better qualification for Heaven? Why should really wicked people go to Heaven after what they've done?

What has a man dying 2,000 years ago got to do with today?, which is a question I was asked myself.

A humanistic approach thinks salvation should be based on good works. Doing good is of course commendable but not as a works-based alternative to faith.

Unfortunately, the Bible tells us that all our good deeds are as good as filthy rags:

> *We are all infected and impure with sin. When we display our righteous deeds, they are nothing but filthy rags.*
>
> (Isaiah 64:6 NLT)

There is absolutely nothing you can do to earn your salvation.

God requires a different way—faith.

> *Since God in his wisdom saw to it that the world would never know him through human wisdom, he has used our foolish preaching to save those who believe. It is foolish to the Jews, who ask for signs from heaven. And it is foolish to the Greeks, who seek human wisdom. So, when we*

> *preach that Christ was crucified, the Jews are offended and the Greeks say it's all nonsense.*

But to those who are called by God to salvation, both Jews and Gentiles. *Christ is the power of God and the wisdom of God.* (1 Corinthians 1:21–24 NLT)

God in His wisdom has chosen to make it a matter of faith and not good works. That's why it's called amazing grace, because none of us deserve the free gift of salvation and eternal life. That's why Jesus came in a human body to be the perfect sacrifice the Father would accept.

> *Because God's children are human beings—made of flesh and blood—the Son also became flesh and blood. For only as a human being could he die, and only by dying could he break the power of the devil, who had the power of death. Only in this way could he set free all who have lived their lives as slaves to the fear of dying.* (Hebrews 2:14–15 NLT)

It is actually only the certainty of Heaven that can remove the fear of death and all believers should be able to say, like Paul:

> *For to me, living means living for Christ, and dying is even better. But if I live, I can do more fruitful work for Christ. So, I really don't know which is better. I am torn between the two desires: I long to go and be with Christ, which would be far better for me.*
>
> (Philippians 1:21–23 NLT)

Of course we want to see our children and grandchildren grow up, but to know that a better future awaits us should mean that we look forward to that time with expectation rather than trepidation.

CHAPTER SIX

THE FUTURE

THE BIBLE LAYS out a time framework, right from the beginning at creation, to the close of the age. A brief summary here will help to understand the context of much of what Jesus said, referring back to the Law and the Prophets and looking forward to the close of the age.

God creates the heavens and the earth, and places the first human beings there.

Over time the population grows enormously, but they reject God, causing destruction by a global flood, for which there is plenty of evidence even today.

God calls Abraham to move to a land He will give him and his descendants (Israel) and calls the Jews His own special people.

They end up in Egypt for 400 years, and are then led back to the Promised Land by Moses who gives them the Ten Commandments (the Law).

They are ruled by a series of prophets but demand a king, so have Saul, the first king, followed by David. A long line of good and bad kings follow.

During this time God sent them prophets to call the nation back to Himself, and they prophesied the coming of the Messiah (Hebrew) or Christ (Greek) who would be the King of the Jews.

When Jesus came, to fulfil those prophecies, the Jews rejected Him and crucified Him.

But that's not the end of God's plan. Here we are, 2,000 years later, about to witness the events both prophesied by Jesus and revealed in the Book of Revelation.

The key to understanding prophecy is all about timing. Because Jesus was, and is, the King of The Jews, because they rejected Him first time round, He's coming back to literal Israel to establish His Kingdom.

If this all sounds a bit far-fetched think of it this way: God is so totally committed to His

Word that every unfulfilled prophecy must be fulfilled and any promise made must be kept.

When God promised Abraham the land defined in Genesis 15:18 as being from the river of Egypt to the great river, the River Euphrates, He is obligated to keep that promise. As it's never happened yet it will most definitely happen when Jesus returns. Again, this may sound far-fetched in our modern social media age, but if God says it will happen, then it will!

> *Now when He had spoken these things, while they watched, He was taken up, and a cloud received Him out of their sight. And while they looked steadfastly toward Heaven as He went up, behold, two men stood by them in white apparel, who also said, "Men of Galilee, why do you stand gazing up into heaven? This same Jesus, who was taken up from you into heaven, will so come in like manner as you saw Him go into heaven."* (Acts 1:9–11)

The return of the Lord, sometimes called The Second Coming or The Second Advent, is clearly there in the Bible. Unsurprisingly, the disciples quizzed Him when all this would happen.

> *"Take heed that no one deceives you. For many will come in My name, saying, 'I am the Christ', and will deceive many. And you will hear of wars and rumors of wars. See that you are not troubled; for all these things must come to pass, but the end is not yet. For nation will rise against nation, and kingdom against kingdom. And there will be famines, pestilences, and earthquakes in various places. All these are the beginning of sorrows."*
>
> (Matthew 24:5–8)

I am writing this during the war in Ukraine, the greatest war in Europe since 1945. One consequence is likely to be famine in countries who rely on Ukrainian grain, which cannot easily be exported to countries who rely on it. Other crops such as sunflower oil are affected too, as well as agricultural fertilizer which used to be exported.

We also face global warming and the lack of rain is affecting harvests worldwide. We have also had swarms of locusts in east Africa devouring crops on a massive scale. We've just about come out of Covid 19, but more pestilences are likely. We've just had another recent earthquake in Afghanistan, killing over 1,000 people.

So, it looks like we're in the season Jesus warned us about. Setting dates is incredibly difficult, and those who've tried inevitably have been shown to be wrong. But we are told to discern the times and seasons.

So why does this matter? The simple answer is because we live in a fragile dangerous world where life and prosperity are not certain anymore.

We have to be right with God, because our tiny lifespan on earth determines our eternal future.

> *Then He spoke a parable to them, saying:*
>
> *"The ground of a certain rich man yielded plentifully. And he thought within himself, saying, 'What shall I do since I have no room to store my crops?' So, he said, 'I will do this: I will pull down my barns and build greater, and there I will store all my crops and goods.*
>
> *And I will say to my soul, "Soul, you have many goods laid up for many years; take your ease; eat, drink and be merry."' But*

> *God said to him,*
>
> *'Fool! This night your soul will be required of you; then whose will those things be which you have provided?'*
>
> *"So is he who lays up treasure for himself, and is not rich toward God."*
>
> (Luke 12:16–21)

So here we are, in a dangerous world, with no certainty of even being alive tomorrow, moving into a season Jesus warned us about.

CHAPTER SEVEN

THE BOOK OF REVELATION

THE REASON THIS book is important is because it relates to a future that will most likely happen in our lifetime. Despite others believing that in past centuries the evidence of being in this season is all around.

The Apostle John is given this vision on the island of Patmos.

It starts with a warning to seven churches that if they didn't repent Jesus would remove Himself from them. Well, they didn't and none of them exist today.

There are then a series of judgements on the earth, seven seals followed by seven bowls (judgments). What's significant is that whereas men and women could repent and be saved instead

> *They blasphemed the God of heaven because of their pains and their sores, and did not repent of their deeds.*
>
> (Revelation 16:13)

God's purpose in all this is to get men to repent—but they won't! So, things get progressively worse.

John is then given a vision of the great white throne judgement. I'm presenting it here because once again it emphasises ultimate accountability.

> *And I saw a great white throne and the one sitting on it. The earth and the sky fled from his presence, but they found no place to hide. I saw the dead, both great and small, standing before God's throne. And the books were opened, including the Book of Life. And the dead were judged according to what they had done, as recorded in the books. The sea gave up its*

> *dead, and death and the grave gave up their dead. And all were judged according to their deeds. Then death and the grave were thrown into the lake of fire. This lake of fire is the second death. And anyone whose name was not found recorded in the Book of Life was thrown into the lake of fire.* (Revelation 20:11–15 NLT)

So, it is pretty important that your name is in the Lamb's Book of Life.

> *Then I saw a new heaven and a new earth, for the old heaven and the old earth had disappeared.*
>
> (Revelation 21:1 NLT)

This is significant because we have utterly trashed the earth, so God will create a new earth for believers to live in, as earth is the perfect environment for us. It's a second Garden of Eden this time sin and sickness free for ever.

Why a new Heaven? Because there was war in the first Heaven and the devil and all his demons needed to be thrown out and God's way is not to patch things up but start afresh.

So, back to the question: What will you do when you're dead?

The answer clearly depends on whether you have personally repented and asked God to forgive you, and trusted in Christ as the one who died on the cross for your sin.

Some of the stuff I've written about is truly horrific, but having read about it you can avoid it! In fact, the Bible tells us:

> *The Lord is not slack concerning His promise, as some count slackness, but is longsuffering toward us, not willing that any should perish but that all should come to repentance.* (2 Peter 3:9).

That's the key. Your destination can be Heaven if you make that decision.

Don't dismiss what you've read. This stuff is real and will affect all of us, whether we believe it or not. There is an amazing future for those who love God and trust in Jesus as their personal savior. Please be one of them!

Finally, here's a prayer you could make your own:

> Dear God, I acknowledge my sin, that I have broken your laws, and I will turn around and trust You that You forgive those who truly repent.

Thank you that Jesus died in my place for my sin.

I receive Your forgiveness as a free gift and ask you to fill me with the Holy Spirit and give me the assurance that my name is in the Book of Life and that my eternal destiny will be with Jesus in the new Heaven and new Earth.

Amen.

For God so loved the world that He gave His only begotten Son, that whoever believes in Him should not perish but have everlasting life. (John 3:16)

ALSO AVAILABLE FROM BRIDGE-LOGOS

THE OVERCOMING LIFE

D. L. Moody

"The world, the flesh, and the devil are too much for any man," Moody says. "But if we are linked to Christ by faith . . . we shall get the victory over every enemy."

This classic includes *The Way to God,* a companion book he wrote in 1884, in which he lovingly instructs Christians on how to draw nearer to God and warns against backsliding. These books, along with other rare, shorter Moody works and a riveting biography comprise this truly compelling volume.

ISBN: 978-0-88270-400-5

Well-known as The Evangelist of the Nineteenth Century, Dwight Lyman Moody (1837-1899) lived out his passion to preach the gospel with humility, simplicity and power to a lost and dying world—leading sinners to the Savior and equipping them as His disciples.

BRIDGE LOGOS

ALSO AVAILABLE FROM BRIDGE-LOGOS

PRACTICAL RELIGION

by J. C. Ryle

Compilation and Biography by Gene Fedele

Practical Religion, by J. C. Ryle was first published in 1878 and is renowned as a theological and apologetic Christian "classic"—esteemed for its clear, profoundly growing and penetrating narrative on the practice of genuine Christian living. Within its pages, Ryle masterfully unfolds practical biblical truths in a series of papers written to address critical aspects of where personal faith in Christ and the practice of that faith in holy living unite and are essential for Christian growth and effectiveness as a witness for Christ in the world. Ryle's unique style penetrates the heart and challenges the mind of its readers, not for the faint of heart. No wonder Charles Spurgeon called him "an evangelical champion."

ISBN: 978-1-61036-264-1

Facebook.com/genefedele

BRIDGE LOGOS

ALSO AVAILABLE FROM BRIDGE-LOGOS

LET THEM HEAR MOSES

Ray Comfort

Explore the book of Exodus as we discover how the achievements and principles of Moses can be applied into our daily lives today. Just as Moses was used by God to lead the Israelites out of slavery into the promised land, God calls us to do the same in our generation.

ISBN: 9781610362177

SCIENTIFIC FACTS IN THE BIBLE

Ray Comfort

Most people, even Christians, don't know that the Bible contains a wealth of incredible scientific, medical, and prophetic facts. That being so, the implications are mind boggling.

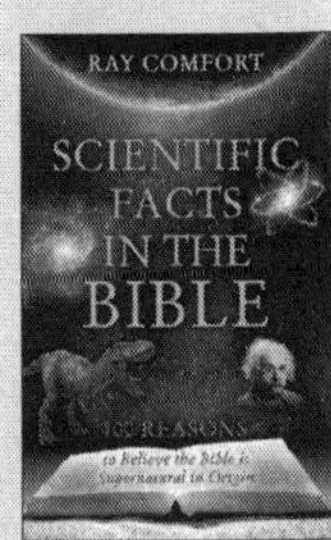

ISBN: 9780882708799

HOW TO KNOW GOD EXISTS

Ray Comfort

Does God exist, or does He not? In this compelling book, Ray Comfort argues the case with simple logic and common sense. This book will convince you that belief in God is reasonable and rational—a matter of fact and not faith.

ISBN: 9780882704326

ALSO AVAILABLE FROM BRIDGE-LOGOS

SCHOOL OF BIBLICAL EVANGELISM

Ray Comfort, Kirk Cameron, and Mark Spence

ISBN: 9780882709680

This comprehensive study offers 101 lessons on thought-provoking topics including basic Christian doctrines, cults and other religions, creation/evolution, and more. Learn how to share your faith simply, effectively, and biblically . . . the way Jesus did.

WAY OF THE MASTER STUDENT EDITION

Ray Comfort & Allen Atzbi

ISBN: 9781610364737

Youth today are being inundated with opposing messages, and desperately need to hear the truth of the gospel. How can you reach them? Sharing the good news is much easier than you think . . . by using some timeless principles.

BRIDGE LOGOS

ALSO AVAILABLE FROM BRIDGE-LOGOS

SEARCH N RESCUE

Eddie Roman

Search N Rescue is a practical guide to reaching people with the good news of Jesus Christ. Eddie has been teaching evangelism classes and leading outreaches for the past six years. As producer/director of Ray Comfort and Kirk Cameron's TV show, The Way of the Master, Eddie knows how to communicate deep truths in a way that is easy to grasp. Many Christians want to share the gospel with friends and family, but few actually do. Fear of rejection stifles many. Others don't share Christ because they don't know what to say. Drawing insight from the Bible as well as personal experience, Eddie gives clear instruction on how to overcome the obstacles and share your faith.

ISBN: 978-1-61036-216-0

eddieroman.com

BRIDGE LOGOS